Original title:
Christmas Dreams and Hopes

Copyright © 2024 Creative Arts Management OÜ
All rights reserved.

Author: Ethan Prescott
ISBN HARDBACK: 978-9916-94-054-9
ISBN PAPERBACK: 978-9916-94-055-6

Winter Wishes on the Edge of Time

Snowflakes dance like tiny elves,
Tickling noses, spinning shelves.
Hot cocoa spills on my warm feet,
The cat thinks it's a tasty treat.

Gifts wrapped tight in paper bright,
A pair of socks, oh what a sight!
A sweater with a dog on front,
I wear it proud, and none can stunt.

Lights are twinkling, strung with care,
Grandpa's snores are quite the air!
Reindeer snacks are just stale bread,
The dog's convinced it's time for bed.

Snowmen wobble, noses askew,
Carrots missing, oh what a crew!
I'd trade a gift for some warm pie,
With whipped cream clouds that make me sigh.

Lanterns of Hope in the Glistening Snow

In the night, a snowman grins wide,
His carrot nose on a wild sleigh ride.
With a scarf that's twisted, he looks quite sassy,
His friends all laugh, saying, 'Isn't he classy?'

Hot cocoa spills, like a wintery spree,
Marshmallows bob like a jolly decree.
I swear the cookies just winked at me,
Maybe it's magic, or just pure glee!

Enchanted Echoes of the Season

Elves in pajamas, making a mess,
Looping the lights, such a tangled press.
Santa's on break, sipping on cheer,
While reindeer are prancing, sipping root beer.

Snowflakes twirl, like dancers of glee,
While I slip and fall, oh why can't I see?
The cat in a box, just made his own throne,
It's a holiday circus, but somehow I'm prone!

Tides of Warmth in the Cold

Socks on a snowman? What a sight to behold,
As twinkling lights dance, both brave and bold.
Pine trees shake off the wintery chill,
And mice might be plotting a holiday thrill.

Jingle bells ringing in a cat's joyful chase,
While sugar cookies vanish without a trace.
A snowball fight turns into a pie,
And laughter erupts—oh, my, oh my!

Hearts Adrift in a Sea of Snowflakes

A gingerbread house that's leaning in style,
Sweet frosting walls, we'll fix it in a while.
Kids zoom past, on their bright colored sleds,
Crafting snow forts where laughter spreads.

Fluffy hats wobble on heads in a row,
As snowflakes fall, tossing sparkles below.
Each snowman's a legend crafted with flair,
But why does mine look like it doesn't care?

Flickering Lights and Warm Embraces

Twinkling bulbs dance on the tree,
While cats plot mischief, oh so free.
Grandma's fruitcake, a sight to dread,
We laugh as we nibble, wishing for bread.

Santa's sleigh gets stuck in the snow,
Reindeer snicker, 'Oh no, not that go!'
Hot cocoa spills on the carpet bright,
A marshmallow snowball fight ignites the night.

Sleigh Bells Ringing Through the Silence

Sleigh bells jingle; the dog starts to bark,
A neighbor's attempt at caroling—oh, what a lark!
We sneak holiday snacks in a festive race,
But dad's 'Secret Stash' is the best hiding place.

Wrapping gifts with tape in a sticky mess,
A paper cut leads to a holiday stress.
We giggle and squawk as the ribbon flies,
'This gift's from the puppy!' a sweet little lie.

Echoes of Joy in Frosted Air

Snowflakes tumble, they land on my nose,
My snowman wobbles, he almost doze.
This scarf is knotted, I'm stuck with a grin,
Watch out for birds—they're aiming to win!

Mittens mismatched, a colorful clash,
We slide down the hill, it's a glorious splash.
Next door's cat looks on, with a tilt of its head,
As we cheerfully bounce, face-first in the spread.

The Gift of a Silent Night

The lights go dim, we whisper and stare,
Is that a elf? No, just dad's wild hair!
The clock strikes twelve, shouts echo with cheer,
As we start trading socks—hilarious year!

Gifts wrapped in paper, a beautiful sight,
But scissors are banned—they have joined in the fight.
As laughter erupts in this cozy old den,
We dream of more chaos—let the fun begin!

Canvas of Dreams in Icy Shades

In the frosty air we play,
A snowman's hat, gone astray.
His carrot nose begins to droop,
As snowflakes form a merry loop.

Children giggle, all in a row,
Sledding down with a loud "Whoah!"
Hot cocoa spilled on the way down,
A chocolate smile instead of a frown.

A Yearning for the Fire's Glow

The candles flicker, shadows dance,
A few popped corn for a merry chance.
Uncle Joe spills his favorite drink,
As Aunt Sue's fruitcake makes us think.

We gather 'round with warm and cheer,
But Grandma's cat just stole a beer.
Laughter echoes in the cozy nook,
As we dodge the oddball, sneaky cook.

Joys Fluttering with the Snowflakes

Outside the flurries swirl and twist,
While kids throw snowballs with a twist.
A friendly war breaks out with glee,
As giggles bounce from tree to tree.

Frosty noses, rosy cheeks,
Sledding tales, the laughter peaks.
We fall in piles, a jumbled heap,
Snow angels made, oh what a leap!

A Gathering Beneath the Evergreen

Under the tree, we find the stash,
Wrappings torn with a joyful crash.
A rubber chicken, oh what a sight,
Makes Grandpa laugh on this chilly night.

The lights twinkle, we sing a song,
But Dad forgot the words, all wrong!
As cookies vanish at lightning speed,
We catch the crumbs, there's always greed.

Glimmers of Hope in Winter's Embrace

When snowmen wobble with their carrot noses,
And kids throw snowballs, avoiding cold poses.
The twinkling lights flicker, a festive glow,
While squirrels search for nuts in the soft snow.

The cocoa's too hot, yet we sip with glee,
Chasing chilly chills, just you and me.
With dreams of warmth in the frosty night,
We'll laugh till we stumble, hearts feeling light.

A Quilt of Love on a Frosty Night

Under covers thick, we snuggle up tight,
While kittens plot mischief in the dim light.
Hot pies on the windowsill make us grin,
But the cat steals a slice, oh, where do we begin?

As frost paints the glass with a delicate sweep,
We giggle and chat while the world's fast asleep.
A patchwork of laughter fills the warm air,
Spreading joy like confetti, everywhere!

The Dance of Shadows and Light

With shadows of reindeer prancing outside,
And shadows of spice cake trying to hide.
We deck the halls with ribbons and cheer,
While Grandma's lost glasses are nowhere near.

As candles get lit and the windowpanes fog,
We peek out to see if it might just be a dog.
Oh, how the laughter fills every room,
In the dance of the season, we all feel the bloom.

Heartbeats Beneath the Mistletoe

Under the sprigs, we brace for a peck,
But Uncle Joe slips and gets stuck in a wreck.
Laughter erupts as we all chime in,
Grinning at chaos through thick and thin.

As carolers sing their off-key tunes,
We tap our feet to the sound of the moons.
With hearts full of joy and silly delight,
We'll prance through the night, till first morning light.

A Time for Miracles Unfolding

A jolly old man broke my roof,
With a laugh like a tune, indeed that was proof.
Reindeer are parked on my lawn with flair,
They really should learn to take better care.
The cookies I baked, they vanished so fast,
If only my waistline would follow the past.
Santa's sleigh got a lift from my dog,
Now he barks at the moon, just like a fog.

The Gift of Light in Darkness

The lights on the house could guide a ship,

Neighbors stop by just to take a dip.

My cat thinks the tree is a new jungle gym,

With ornaments flying, oh, what a whim!

My uncle's bad jokes make everyone cringe,

But they're served with the eggnog, a festive binge.

Yet in this chaos, joy finds a way,

Like a snowman who melted, then danced in the spray.

Evergreen Promises Wrapped in Ribbons

The wrapping paper is the cat's new toy,

He's also unwrapped a whole bin of joy.

With bows in the air and kids on the run,

It's like a parade, but with less fun!

Socks were exchanged, oh what a surprise,

When it's nine feet wide, don't expect any ties.

Grandma's fruitcake still holds its ground,

Like a brick of mystery, we all gather 'round.

Carols in the Heart of Winter

We gathered around with a song and a mug,

But my voice went off like a tired old bug.

Jingle bells ring, and so do the phone,

From relatives asking if we've lost our tone.

The snowflakes fall like confetti at night,

Somehow they gleam, but give us a fright.

We dance in our socks, on this frosty floor,

Laughing so hard till we can't take anymore.

Riding on the Winds of Wonderment

In a sleigh pulled by reindeer, I zoom through the air,
With a jolly old fellow who doesn't seem to care.
He's stuffing his face with a cookie or two,
Laughing and chuckling while I shout, "Woo-hoo!"

With a wink and a nudge, he takes off his hat,
A squirrel comes scurrying, asking for that!
"Can I have a ride?" he squeaks with delight,
But the reindeer just snicker and take to their flight.

We pass by a snowman, a wiggle-bellied sight,
Who claims he can moonwalk, but slides left and right.
He waves at the penguins who tumble and spin,
"Let's boogie till dawn!" they squawk with a grin.

So here we are flying, a hilarious crew,
With laughter and mischief in all that we do.
On this wild winter ride, we'll not lose our cheer,
Who knew winter wishes could bring such good beer?

Voices of the Season in Harmony

Bells are ringing loudly, a cat starts to yowl,
A choir in the corner, singing, what a howl!
The dog joins the chorus, howling with flair,
Even the goldfish tries to wiggle in air.

With jingle bells jingling, they scatter the tunes,
While the kid in the corner is bouncing like balloons.
"Oh, listen to us!" the squirrel exclaims,
As he dances around with his acorn games.

The tree lights are twinkling like stars up above,
And a mouse in a bowtie is looking for love.
He sings a sweet serenade, quite off-key,
While a toaster serenades with a pop and a spree.

So gather 'round closely, let's throw in a cheer,
For the quirkiest voices that we get to hear.
Together we'll laugh till we snort and we wheeze,
These unlikely musicians put us all at ease.

The Magic in the Stillness of Night

As the moon takes its throne in the velvet sky,
A llama in pajamas wanders by, oh my!
He's munching on shadows and counting sheep,
Whispering secrets as the world slips to sleep.

A raccoon in a top hat steals cookies with glee,
While the owl just hoots, "You won't catch me!"
The stars are all twinkling, mischievous and bright,
Playing hide and seek till the dawn's early light.

Yet somewhere in quiet, a wonder unfurls,
A snowball fight breaks out with a flurry of pearls.
Snowflakes are giggling, the trees are aglow,
As laughter drifts softly on the chill winter's blow.

So let us remember the tales of the night,
Of creatures and antics that brought us delight.
In the hush of the hour, where mischief takes flight,
The magic within is the glow of moonlight.

Silent Wishes Beneath the Stars

Under glittering skies, we make our own luck,
With a cat in a scarf and a very tight truck.
The stars sprinkle hopes like confetti so bright,
While a hedgehog on roller skates zooms out of sight.

A wish on a shooting star flies with a grin,
But the raccoon takes aim—oh, there goes a bin!
Our laughter erupts as we dodge flying pies,
As the night fills with joy and sweet, silly sighs.

So here's to the wonders that whirl around us,
With marshmallow clouds and a dash of good fuss.
Though wishes may scatter like crumbs in the night,
We'll cherish the moments, oh, what a delight!

With silent desires wrapped up like a gift,
We're a troupe of misfits in a whimsical drift.
So let's twirl in our dreams, with laughter and cheer,
For the magic of night-time keeps us all near.

Whispers of Winter's Eve

In the frosty air, we laugh and cheer,
As snowflakes dance, it's that time of year.
The cat in a hat, oh what a sight,
Chasing his tail in pure delight.

With mugs of cocoa, we giggle and sip,
As marshmallows bounce, it's a sweet little trip.
The tree lights twinkle, like stars in a haze,
While Uncle Joe snores through the festive craze.

Starlit Wishes on Snowy Nights

Outside is a blanket, all fluffy and white,
While we build a snowman that's almost a fright.
Carrot for nose, and a hat that's too small,
He wobbles a bit but we're having a ball.

The dogs all are barking, and kids squeal with glee,
As sleds go flying down mountains, whee!
But one little trip leaves us laughing too loud,
When Dad tumbles down, oh he's so very proud!

A Hearth of Love and Light

By the fire we gather, with tales in our minds,
Of reindeer who dance and leave gifts behind.
The cookie sneaks vanish, oh what a treat,
While Grandpa sneaks bites, oh isn't he sweet?

The stockings are hung, a few with a clatter,
When Auntie spills eggnog, oh what a matter!
With laughter and giggles, the night's full of cheer,
We can't wait for tomorrow, for sweet surprise near.

The Promise of December's Magic

In a world made of sugar, and spice, oh so nice,
Cookies and laughter are free with a slice.
The elves in the workshop all spark with delight,
As mischief and giggles drift into the night.

With jingles and tinkles, they prance about,
While Santa gets stuck, and we hear him shout!
From rooftops to chimneys, the stories unfold,
As we gather round, with warmth to behold.

Dreams Adrift on Gentle Snowflakes

A snowman wobbles, quite a sight,
His carrot nose is slightly tight.
With twiggy arms, he reveals his flaws,
But who can frown when winter draws?

Sledding down hills, we shriek with glee,
A wild ride, can't stop, oh me!
Rolling in snow, we play tag with fate,
Too cold to care, we laugh, then skate!

Hot cocoa spills, marshmallows afloat,
A steamy drink in a flimsy boat.
With each sip, a frothy cheer,
We dream of sugar plums, oh dear!

Frosty flakes tickle our noses bright,
As we squint at the shimmering night.
Under twinkling lights, we jump and spin,
Oh, what a joy—let the fun begin!

The Joyful Spirit of Giving

Presents wrapped in shiny foil,
Unruly ribbons, oh what a toil!
My cat's in the box, claiming his space,
As I wrestle with tape, a silly chase!

Cookies baked with an extra dash,
Oops! That flour makes quite the splash.
A sprinkle fight soon ensues, it's true,
Joyful chaos in my holiday brew!

Knocking on doors with treats galore,
A tango of laughter outside, we roar.
Gift exchanges become a sly game,
Who's got the best? Oh, who can name?

The joy in sharing, we all agree,
Is better than simply spending a fee.
With giggles and grins, we spread the cheer,
For 'tis the season to hold joy near!

A Sanctuary of Love and Laughter

A cozy hearth, where all is bright,
Grandma's stories take flight at night.
We roast marshmallows with sticky hands,
While Uncle Joe breaks into silly bands!

Laughter echoes through the festive hall,
Dad dresses up, looking quite the fool,
With elf ears on and a reindeer hat,
He's our jolly king, and we all clap!

Games get heated, who can keep score?
The prize? A hug—can't ask for more!
Snowflakes dance; while hearts unite,
In a joyful huddle, oh what a sight!

With love surrounding, there's no need for fuss,
In our merry sanctuary, it's all about us.
Finding joy in every silly thing,
Laughter is the gift that keeps on giving!

Midnight Wishes on Softly Falling Snow

Under the moon, where dreams take flight,
Snowflakes whisper secrets of the night.
Half-asleep, I wish for magic,
Hoping to find the strange and tragic!

The Christmas tree sparkles, a twinkling sight,
The cat is plotting, with mischief delight.
I peek through the window, a silent vow,
To catch a glimpse of the jolly snowplow!

The snowball battles begin in glee,
And giggles erupt, as wild as can be.
With each throw, laughter goes higher,
Such perfect moments make hearts aspire.

Under soft blankets, we dream well and deep,
Of penguins in suits that make us laugh and leap.
So here's to wishes, both silly and grand,
In snowy nights, we joyfully stand!

A Journey to the North Star

Off we go with goofy grins,
Riding reindeer, let the fun begin.
With a map all scribbled, bold and bright,
We'll find that star, oh what a sight!

Snowflakes dance, they swirl and twirl,
With giggles loud, and laughter's whirl.
The North Star beckons, we can't sit still,
It's a wobbly ride, but we get our thrill!

Santa's sleigh, what a funny boat,
Bouncing up and down, like a rubber boat.
Elves are hiding, they jump and shout,
"Who wants hot cocoa? Come on, no doubt!"

So we chase the star, each twist, each turn,
With wishes and giggles, oh how we yearn.
For silly moments, bright and clear,
In our sparkling hearts, we spread the cheer!

Cocoa and Comfort Under the Stars

Gather 'round, the mugs are hot,
Marshmallows jumping, oh what a lot!
Sipping cocoa, with a grin so wide,
Under the starlight, we won't hide!

Whispers of wishes float with the steam,
While silly one-liners make the group beam.
The night is young, with a playful cheer,
Laughter bubbles up, forget all fear!

We build a fort, with blankets galore,
A cozy haven, who could ask for more?
S'mores in hand, and stories to share,
While starlits giggle, as we lay bare!

So lift your mugs, here's to the night,
With cocoa hugs, everything feels right.
Friendship and joy, under twinkling skies,
Our hearts are aglow, it's no surprise!

Pinecones and the Spirit of Giving

Pinecones rolling down the street,
Creating chaos with little feet.
We gather them up, a million in sight,
Crafting our gifts, oh, what delight!

Wrapping them up in paper so bright,
Tied with wild ribbons, what a sight!
Our fingers are sticky from glue and fun,
Hoping our gifts will be number one!

Neighbors peeking out, they start to grin,
"What's all the laughter? Where do we begin?"
We wave them closer, come join our spree,
Let's spread the cheer, just you and me!

So here's a toast to surprises galore,
In our hearts, we know there's always more.
With pinecones and giggles, we'll paint the town,
Planting seeds of joy, wearing smiles, not a frown!

Chasing Shadows of the Past

In a pine-scented memory, we sneak,
Following shadows, giggling, cheek to cheek.
They dance around like playful sprites,
Leading us to those whimsical nights.

The past is funny, like a wobbly toy,
With laughter that bursts like a bright little joy.
Old tales are told around a flickering flame,
Mimicking accents, oh, what a game!

We search for the moments that made us smile,
Each silly incident adding to our pile.
With a wink and a nod, we dig in deep,
Finding treasures of laughter, they make us leap!

So here's to the shadows, our friends from the years,
They tickle our hearts, wipe away fears.
With every echo, we giggle with glee,
In this merry chase, we're wild and free!

Sleigh Bells Whispering Through the Night

Sleigh bells jingle, what a sound,
Rooftops echo, laughter found.
Reindeer dancing, prancing too,
Maybe they'll join us for a brew!

Snowflakes swirl, a frosty cheer,
Elves are giggling, spreading beer.
Santa's lost his left shoe here,
Does he trip on dreams, I fear?

Cookies vanish, crumbs in tow,
Rats are feasting, stealing the show.
Milk is now a chocolate flood,
Last I checked, it was just a dud!

Hopes and wishes float like kites,
Comets zoom with festive lights.
Cocoa spills, oh what a sight,
Cozy chaos through the night!

The Lantern's Glow of Tomorrow

Lanterns flicker, shadows play,
Wishing on stars that drift away.
Mice are creeping with their spoils,
Stealing snacks from human coils.

Tomorrow's pie might not exist,
Thanks to fluffs with tiny fists!
Gingersnap thieves in a spree,
Do they dream of making tea?

Wreaths are spinning, round and round,
Laughter echoes, joy is found.
Each silly prank brings a smile,
Candles drip like they're in style!

Two mice chase, as shadows blink,
In the lantern's glow, we think.
Tomorrow's hopes, a vibrant glow,
In this silliness, let us grow!

Frosted Fantasies on Winter's Breeze

Frosty windows, secret sights,
Noses pressed for magical nights.
Snowballs fly, a playful fight,
Frosty dreams take off in flight!

Socks are hanging, but beware,
One got stuffed with cat's old hair.
Whispers of snowmen joining in,
Rubber ducks, they grace our din!

Bells are ringing, a marching band,
Who knew they could play so grand?
Snowmen giggle, losing their hats,
Hiding treats in roving rats!

Wishes bundled up so tight,
In the frosted morning light.
What is real, and what's a tease?
Frosted fantasies on winter's breeze!

Enchanted Nights in a Snowy Haze

In the night, so wondrous bright,
Mice wear hats, a comical sight.
Candles flicker, casting spells,
In this chaos, we all dwell.

Snowflakes dance, they spin around,
Elves are sneaking snacks they've found.
Candy canes with giggly grace,
Wobbling all over the place!

Cozy blankets piled up high,
Underneath, a secret pie.
Whispers fill the frosty air,
What to eat? Oh, do we care?

Nights enchanted, full of glee,
In the snow, we're wild and free.
With laughter ringing, chill and haze,
We embrace these funny days!

A Journey Through the Winter's Dreamscape

As snowflakes dance and swirl so bright,
I trip on my boots, what a funny sight!
The reindeer chuckle as I tumble down,
In this frosty land, I'm the jester of town.

Chasing snowmen with noses of carrots,
They wobble and laugh, oh how they inherit!
A sleigh full of gifts, but I just want pie,
So I sneak a slice while the elf looks awry.

The stars above twinkle like mischief and cheer,
Whispers of laughter fill the brisk atmosphere.
With hot cocoa spills and marshmallows afloat,
I dream of a winter wrapped in a goat!

A snowball fight breaks, it's pure chaos and fun,
I'm hit by a toddler, oh boy, I can run!
We laugh until tears freeze right on our face,
In this quirky season, we quicken our pace.

Whispers of Joy Beneath the Boughs

Underneath the branches, we laughed and we played,
A squirrel stole my hat, what a sneaky charade!
With pinecone adornments just like little gems,
We dance in the snow, joined by frosty friends.

The cat draped in tinsel acts like a queen,
While I hold a sprig, but it's stuck like a scene.
Elf boots on cats, oh, what a surprise,
As they prance in delight, my laughter just flies!

The cookies I baked are now just a smear,
My dog took a bite, oh, he has no fear!
Strutting around with crumbs on his snout,
In this festive caper, there's never a doubt.

With twinkling lights and slightly bowed heads,
Our giggles ignite as we share silly threads.
Through whispers of joy, in the cool winter night,
We find warmth in laughter, what a splendid sight!

Rejoicing in Simple Moments

In lines at the store, we shuffle and sway,
A kid in a cart tosses snowballs our way.
With laughter contagious in this merry parade,
I slip on a present, oh, what a charade!

Hot cider's a must, but where is my mug?
The puppy found it—he's pulled me a rug!
We gather 'round fires with marshmallow sticks,
As stories unravel, oh, the funny mix!

The tree is quite crooked, it leans like a drunk,
But it's sparkly magic, from trunk to the trunk.
With baubles balancing like acrobats brave,
We cheer for our quirks, see how we behave!

In simple delights, we toast to the night,
A dance in the living room, oh what a sight!
With joy in our hearts and giggles so wide,
We savor the magic this laughter provides.

The Promise of Tomorrow in the Snow

Tomorrow is snowy, they say with a grin,
But today, I got stuck in a deep pile of sin.
Wrapped like a burrito in blankets and fluff,
I dream of hot chocolate; is that too much stuff?

Outside, there's a ruckus, all children at play,
While I chase my own dreams and keep slipping away.
The snowman just winked; does he know something new?

With a carrot for laughter, he giggles through too.

Each moment whispers soft tales of delight,
Like cats in the tree, oh, what a strange sight!
The plans of tomorrow are snow-dusted dreams,
In the land of the little, nothing's as it seems.

With each stride I take, joy tickles the ground,
My wishes take flight, like the snowflakes around.
So let's dance through the winter, with laughter so bright,

For tomorrow's surprises are tucked in the light!

Lullabies for Winter's Children

Snowflakes dance in twinkling light,
Silly hats and scarves feel just right.
While reindeer prance and giggle with glee,
The snowman winks at you and me.

Chubby cheeks all aglow,
Sledding down hills in quite a row.
Hot cocoa spills on pants so bright,
Oh what fun on this winter night!

Through frosty breaths, we share our cheer,
Whispers loud enough for all to hear.
Elves are plotting with mischief in tow,
Wrapping gifts with ribbons that might just blow!

As we snuggle, ho ho ho!
Dreams of marshmallows begin to flow.
In a world where laughter rules the day,
Winter's children dance and play!

A Star-Crossed Wish Upon a Hill

On a hillside, wishes fly,
Snowmen joust as stars wink high.
One spry wish with rosy cheeks,
Claims to be a bird that speaks!

Dances spinning, snowflakes twirl,
While snowy boys around me hurl.
A deer in reindeer antlers prances,
While candy canes lend mischievous glances!

The twinkling lights attract the cats,
Seeking warmth on cozy mats.
Their tiny paws step soft and slow,
Wishing they could steal the show!

But as we giggle at this fun,
And countless pranks are just begun,
Under stars that twinkle bright,
We share our wishes through the night!

The Sweetness of Shared Stories

Gather 'round for tales to tell,
Of how a cookie piñata fell!
Chasing gingerbread on rollerblades,
As merry laughter serenades.

A story where the moonlight glows,
And silly gnomes wear silly clothes.
Wizards 'neath the mistletoe,
Dodge the tangled lights—you'll know!

Naughty cats who sneak a peek,
Finding treats is what they seek!
A dragon wraps its tail so tight,
In a blanket built for coziness at night!

Each smile we share we hold so dear,
With sips of cocoa and festive cheer.
As tales unfold and laughter rings,
The joy of the season endlessly clings!

Imprints of Love on Frosted Ground

Frosty footprints dance along the way,
As we skip and laugh at winter play.
Snowball fights with grinning friends,
Imprints of love that never ends.

A snow angel sprawls—a funny sight,
With floppy wings in snow so white.
Twinkling lights weave laughter's thread,
While snowmen bicker on what's said!

With mittens tangled, we tumble down,
Laughter echoes all over town.
Sledging fast, the speed's a thrill,
And friendship breathes on that snowy hill.

In every print, our hearts align,
Creating stories time can't confine.
With warmth and joy that overflows,
We cherish the love each snowflake shows!

The Countdown of Anticipation

The calendar flips, we cheer,
Anticipation brings us near.
One day left! Just one more bite,
Of cookies hidden out of sight.

Elves are packing, oh what fun,
They seem to race, they seem to run.
Wrapping gifts with paper bright,
Oh, what's in that box tonight?

Tinsel tangled in our hair,
Funny hats that we all wear.
Mittens mismatched, what a sight,
Yet we smile with pure delight.

Soon the bells will ring with glee,
We sing our songs of jubilee.
Laughter echoes, no complaints,
As we await the jolly saints.

Lullabies Beneath the Mistletoe

Under green, we sway and sigh,
A mistletoe hangs up so high.
'Tis a prank for Cousin Fred,
Who thinks he'll find true love instead.

Singing softly, the carols flow,
While Uncle Joe steals all the show.
With a wink and playful jest,
He'll try to hug the family's quest.

Sugar cookies stacked and tall,
Watch it fall! Oh, what a brawl!
Flour fights and frosting fun,
Can we ever be done, oh, none!

As we close our eyes to dream,
We giggle at our silly theme.
Beneath the glow, so softly bright,
Who knew laughter was our light?

Melodies of Hope in a Winter's Tale

In the frosty air we glide,
On rubber boots we take our ride.
With snowball fights and quick retreats,
Our chattering teeth play silly beats.

Songs of cheer float through the breeze,
While Aunt Sue finds it hard to sneeze.
Her nose is red, her cheeks aglow,
As she recites the tales we know.

The snowman wobbles, eyes of coal,
He loses balance, that's our goal!
With carrot noses popping round,
We laugh aloud, no frowns are found.

In winter's tale, we spin and jest,
Finding joy is quite the quest.
With hopes wrapped tight in laughter's fold,
The treasure's worth is more than gold.

Stars that Light the Darkened Sky

Look up high, the stars we see,
Twinkling like our family tree.
"Is that a comet?" we all shout,
As Aunt Emma spins about!

Flashing lights on every house,
There's even one that looks like mouse!
We giggle at the funny sights,
As the neighbors string those lights.

Underneath the midnight glow,
We roast marshmallows, oh what a show!
With sticky fingers, we all share,
Sweet moments tossed into the air.

As we gather, hopes take flight,
Stars above us shine so bright.
With laughter ringing far and wide,
In this magic, we all abide.

A Journey to the Heart of the Night

The stars are twinkling, oh what a sight,
Sleigh bells are ringing, quite late at night.
Rudolph's GPS is lost, what a shame,
He's circling the block, playing the game.

Mrs. Claus is laughing, sipping her tea,
While the elves are searching for missing keys.
A snowman in shorts, what a funny show,
He looks quite confused, but he's ready to go.

The reindeer are dancing in festive delight,
Prancer is leading, all lit up bright.
A twirl and a spin, they're all in their groove,
Even old Dasher just wants to move.

So let's raise a toast, with cocoa so warm,
To the silly adventures that keep us from harm.
In dreams when we frolic through starlit froth,
We'll laugh and we'll giggle, that's how we trot.

The Caress of Snow on Secluded Streets

Oh, the snowflakes are falling, a beautiful mess,
But my nose is all red, I must confess.
With snow in my boots and a grin on my face,
I waddle like penguin, a clumsy old race.

The neighbors are wrapped in a battle of cheer,
Whipping up cookies, come gather near!
But Fido is plotting a heist on the table,
As a sneaky little pooch, he's quite the fable.

The lights that we strung look slightly askew,
Twinkling like stars in a broad daylight view.
A snowman appears with a carrot for nose,
He's sporting a hat that he clearly chose.

We laugh as we stumble through pathways so white,
Joy fills the air, all crafted in bright.
For each fleeting moment brings giggles and cheer,
In a whimsical world, where hope is sincere.

Memory Lane Paved in Snowflakes

Down memory lane with a slip and a slide,
We journey together, come take a ride.
With laughter like sunshine lighting the way,
Every moment's a treasure, come join the play.

The snowball fight starts, oh what a delight,
But someone got hit, and now there's a bite!
Giggles erupt from a plush winter fort,
While mittens are flying in this festive sport.

The trees all are gleaming with joy and with cheer,
But a squirrel in a hat seems to commandeer.
He twirls with a flair, shouting 'I'm the king!'
And the laughter surrounds as the snowflakes take wing.

So let's dance through the flakes, in this magical scene,
With memories made that are bright and serene.
For warmth in our hearts warms the cold winter night,
As we twirl and we play, everything feels right.

Elysian Whispers of the First Frost

The frost has arrived like a mischievous sprite,
Whispering secrets beneath the moonlight.
The trees wear a coat of shimmering white,
While I trip on my scarf, oh what a sight!

The snowflakes are twirling like dancers so bold,
Each one unique, in the wintertime cold.
With cocoa in hand and a marshmallow tower,
We laugh as it topples, what a sweet shower!

The carolers chant with a tune that is bright,
But one lost his voice, oh what a fright!
We hum along slowly, trying to cheer,
While some of us chuckle and share a good beer.

So here's to the frolic, the fun that we find,
In the magic of seasons, and moments that bind.
In whispers of frost, there's a warmth we create,
With laughter inseparable, oh isn't it great!

A Blanket of Stars to Keep Us Warm

Beneath the stars, we laugh and play,
With snowball fights that just won't fray.
A flake on my nose, I giggle and scream,
As we float through this frosty dream.

The rabbit next door just tried to hop,
He tripped and fell; oh, what a crop!
His ears flopped down, he twirled with glee,
Who knew bunnies could dance so free?

Hot cocoa spills on my favorite sock,
The marshmallows melt, oh what a shock!
We toast our mugs, they clang and cheer,
Warming hearts with laughter sincere.

So if you see a snowman stumble,
Just chuckle along, don't you dare grumble.
In the glow of the night, we twirl and spin,
Wrapped in this joy, let the fun begin!

Timeless Tales of Warm Hearts

Old tales told by the fire's bright glow,
Of elves and mishaps we all know.
A cat with a hat? Oh, what a sight!
Prowling around in the soft moonlight.

A turkey that flew, yes, that's no lie!
It soared through the branches, oh my, oh my!
We laughed so hard, our bellies ached,
Who knew Thanksgiving could be so baked?

As stockings hang, so heavy and low,
We sneak candy canes, just us, no foe.
The secrets we share would make you cry,
Underneath the tree, just my friends and I.

So gather 'round, let's share some laughs,
Life's a treasure when friendship we craft.
In these timeless tales, we find our spark,
Warm hearts together, we light up the dark!

The Melody of Joy in the Winter Air

Children singing with voices so bright,
Their little feet dashing left and right.
A puppy joins in, howling a tune,
While Santa's sleigh swoops by the moon.

A frozen pond, we glide and slide,
Dodging each other, we giggle and ride.
A tumble here, a splash over there,
The laughter of winter fills the cold air.

Mittens all mismatched, who cares, I say!
They keep my fingers warm in this ballet.
We spin like tops, our heads feeling free,
In this frosty dance, just you and me.

So let's hum along to this winter's sound,
With each joyful note that we've found.
In this merry madness, we spark and glow,
Creating our melody, letting hearts grow!

Cocoa Dreams Under Twinkling Lights

Here's a cup filled to the brim,
With cocoa topped, oh, what a whim!
Marshmallows float, like clouds on high,
As we sip under the big starry sky.

The lights are tangled, oh what a mess!
A reindeer struts, looking quite fresh.
He winks at me, I blink right back,
With dreams of fudge making me smack.

The carols ring out, we sing off-key,
Our voices get louder, just you and me.
A jolly old elf has slipped on a toy,
Falling with gusto, oh what joy!

So here's to the season, all quirks and cheer,
Bringing together those we hold dear.
With laughter and cocoa, twinkly delight,
We'll make memories that shine ever bright!

When Wishes Wander on Frosty Trails

Snowflakes dance like silly clowns,
Wishes wobble, tumbling down.
A sleigh that sings and talks a bit,
Whispering secrets, oh what a fit!

Elves with mittens, lost their way,
Tripped on gumdrops, what a display!
Rudolph's nose, a disco ball,
Leading us in a merry brawl!

Frosty wears a funky hat,
Mismatched socks and a rubber bat.
Snowmen whistling tunes so bright,
Giggles echo in the night!

Chasing snowflakes, we take a leap,
Finding treasures buried deep.
With every laugh, a wish takes flight,
On frosty trails, we reunite!

Fireside Dreams of Peace and Love

Socks hung high on the mantelpiece,
Chasing shadows, hoping for peace.
Hot cocoa splashes, a marshmallow fight,
The cat's in the tree, it's quite a sight!

Grandma's tales of mischief and fun,
Of a turkey that tried to run.
With every story, our hearts grow warm,
By the fire's glow, we weather the storm.

Popcorn strings dance with great delight,
Celebrating every silly sight.
The dog steals a roll, what a scene,
As laughter fills the room, so keen!

Toasting to moments with silly cheer,
Hoping for mischief in the new year.
With love and joy, we sit and play,
In fireside glow, we spend our day!

Echoes of Laughter in a Winter Wonderland

In the meadow, whispers cheer,
Snowballs fly, let's bring the gear!
Testing sleds that wobble and sway,
Oh, what laughter leads the way!

Snow angels flop like clumsy fish,
Landing with a squish and a squish!
The gingerbread men on the run,
Caught in frosting, oh what fun!

Icicles drip like candy canes,
The dog tries to catch them—what a strain!
With every giggle, the chill subsides,
In this wonderland, joy abides!

As we gather, dance and play,
Creating memories that never fray.
Echoes of laughter, ringing clear,
In this frosty realm, we hold so dear!

Grateful Hearts Gathered Together

Around the table, a feast in view,
Turkey, pies, and a stew or two.
Granddad's jokes, a cheesy parade,
We laugh 'til it's time for charades!

Cousins' antics take center stage,
A holiday play, all the rage.
One forgets lines, the other sings,
Yet somehow, joy is what it brings!

With hats askew and silly cheers,
We toast to love and banish fears.
With smiles wide, we embrace the fun,
Grateful for what this day has spun!

So here's to laughter, love, and cheer,
In this cozy space, we hold dear.
With grateful hearts, our wishes gleam,
In every moment, we find our dream!

The Color of Hope in a Wintry World

In a world dressed in white, what do I see?
A snowman with a scarf, grinning at me.
He winks as he melts, what a sight to behold,
Feeling warmer inside, his laughter is bold.

Little elves on the street, dancing quite spry,
With flippers and shades, oh my oh my!
They juggle hot cocoa, and pies on a plate,
While the cat steals a cookie, oh isn't he great?

Floating balloons shaped like reindeer and stars,
Whirling around cars, over roofs and bars.
With giggles and snickers, the streets are alive,
We'll chase them all down, in our jolly high five.

Under mistletoe fakes, folks kiss and they laugh,
With pies on their heads, what a quirky photograph!
So let's toast to the fun, with cheer in our hearts,
Wishing joy for us all as this wild journey starts!

A Gathering of Hearts on Cold Nights

The wind may be chilly, but we're wrapped up so tight,
In sweaters too big, oh what a sight!
With cocoa and marshmallows, we sit by the glow,
Swapping tales of mischief, and placing bets on the snow.

Grandpa's yarns are taller, like trees in the glade,
Of elves on tall bicycles, heaven made!
While we roll our eyes, there's laughter and cheer,
Sharing hot fudge stories, while sipping our beer!

We argue about socks, who wears them with flair,
As the dog steals the leftovers, without a care.
With giggles and snorts, we hold on to the night,
Till the clock strikes the hour, oh what a delight!

So let's gather around, as the frost starts to bite,
With hearts open wide, everything feels right.
In this crazy old home, the warmth fills the air,
With joy all around us, nothing can compare!

The Echo of Magic in Every Corner

In the attic they found, a hat made of fluff,
With glitter and giggles, it's never enough.
It dances on shelves with a wink and a spin,
Echoing laughter, let the antics begin!

The puppets get feisty, they jump on the floor,
With voices so silly, we all want to roar.
They argue and bicker, the moon shines so bright,
As they pull all the pranks, in the magical light.

There's a tree that's quite shouty, adorned with cracked bells,
It jingles and jangles, as it giggles and yells.
A suggestion of mischief overflows with glee,
As we feast on the cookies, now one for each knee!

With a twist and a whirl, the cheers fill the air,
Sprinkling laughter, a delight to compare.
In every small nook, where mischief does play,
Spreading joy to the world, in a magical way!

Skylines Bedazzled with Light

Up high in the sky, what a humorous scene,
With lights all aglow, like a candy machine.
The stars are out shining, but wait, what's that there?
A squirrel in a sleigh, with a toupee of hair!

The city is bustling, with hats stacked on heads,
While cars in a frenzy, make their jolly threads.
Santa's lost his GPS, oh what a sight,
As he circles the block, looking left, then right!

With tinsel and laughter, we dance in the square,
Counting all of our blessings, and the frosty air.
As the fireworks sparkle, in colors so bright,
We grab all the pie, for a fizzy delight!

So let laughter ring out, till the morning arrives,
With silliness echoing, as joy comes alive.
In this merry old place, with friends near and dear,
We dine on the fun, till the end of the year!

A Tapestry of Twinkling Lights

In a town where snowflakes dance and spin,
A cat in a hat dreams of chubby kin.
He slides down the chimney, a snack in his paw,
Leaving crumbs on the carpet, oh what a flaw!

The reindeer have started their wobbly race,
Tripping over sleigh bells, a hilarious chase.
They giggle and tumble, in glittering shoes,
Who knew holiday cheer could lead to such blues?

Santa's lost track of his own Christmas cheer,
He's stuck in a tree, there's no way to steer!
With a sleigh full of goodies, he shouts, "Oh dear!
Somebody bring me a slice of that pie, right here!"

While stockings hang heavy, with toys packed inside,
A llama munches on the gifts set aside.
The llamas all laugh, with their festive flair,
In this tapestry bright, we find joy everywhere.

Secrets of a Winter's Eve

On a frosty night, secrets twinkle and glow,
As squirrels wear scarves, feeling rather in tow.
They gather up acorns, all dressed up in glee,
Plotting their mischief 'neath the old Christmas tree.

A penguin hops over in bright red a coat,
Announcing his plans to dance, sing, and float.
With each little slip, he wobbles with joy,
While the snowmen applaud, 'Oh that clumsy boy!'

A snowball fight breaks out like festive confetti,
With elves dodging snowflakes, they're quite unsteady.
They sneak and they tumble, with giggles and yelps,
Searching for foes, who are hiding like kelps.

In this winter's tale, laughter fills the air,
With all sorts of magic spun without a care.
As they whisper sweet wishes on frosted glass panes,
We find that these secrets are laughter's loud gains.

Beneath the Tree of Whispers

Beneath the old branches where shadows play tricks,
A raccoon thinks he's found the best candy mix.
He nibbles and munches on sweets from the floor,
While the wise old owl just hoots, "Not the door!"

The gnomes set up camp, singing tunes so absurd,
While squirrels perform what they call 'the third bird.'
With acorn-top hats, they dance round and round,
Their laughter and chaos the best sights abound.

Jingle bells jingle, with a tune that's quite loud,
As a dog wearing antlers leaps into the crowd.
With each clumsy hop, he brings smiles galore,
Don't forget the trouble; there's always much more!

Tomorrow will shine in the glow of delight,
But tonight's all about those giggles and flight.
Beneath the old tree, we'll share in the cheer,
Where dreams often mingle and whimsy is near.

Hearts Alight with Radiant Joy

In a kitchen so busy, the cookies go 'boom!',
As flour-covered kids create holiday gloom.
They laugh and they splatter, all covered in paste,
While mom shakes her head at such delicious waste.

The carolers come with voices so bright,
But trip on the lawn with each jingle bell fright.
They stumble through verses, gets tangled in cheer,
And end up performing a new song, never clear!

A giddy old grandpa attempts the sleigh ride,
His beard is a flurry, he's gone for a glide.
As snow drifts like feathers, he can't help but shout,
"This is the best winter; I'll never back out!"

Hearts dancing wildly, like lights on a string,
In every small echo, the laughter takes wing.
Wrapped in the warmth, we find joy in the coy,
With characters merry and moments of joy.

The Magic of First Snowfall

When flakes drop down like powdered sugar,
And kids rush out, their faces aglow,
Snowmen with carrots and smiles emerge,
While dogs bound in for their frosty show.

Sleds zooming fast down the slippery hill,
Hot cocoa spills on the way to the top,
A snowball fight turns into a thrill,
As laughter and shrieks refuse to stop.

Mittens mismatched and hats askew,
Chasing snowflakes as they swirl in the air,
Trying to catch one, that's the big cue,
But landing face-first in snow, oh beware!

As day fades out and glow lights ignite,
The world sparkles in soft, chilly hush,
With cheeks rosy red from pure delight,
We dance in snow, oh what a big rush!

Wishes Left in Hoarfrost

When morning sun meets frozen dew,
It twinkles bright upon the grass,
A wish written in frosty view,
Yeah, 'I hope my hair doesn't freeze like glass!'

The neighborhood cat on a chilly fence,
Winks with a purr, oh what a scene,
Mice on the run make no defense,
As winter jokes stir our dreams in between.

A hot cup waits on the window sill,
It trembles slightly in the draft,
With your neighbor's duck that loves to spill,
And soon a warm, giggly, good-hearted laugh.

Chasing the snowflakes right and left,
We toss wishes like Santa's list,
Dashing through snow, no time for theft,
At least until someone steps on the mist!

Starry Night's Embrace of Hope

When stars are bright in a velvet sky,
We make wishes on glimmers and glee,
An old tree sways, it seems to sigh,
'What about a pie or two for me?'

Jingle bells ring, but not for long,
As cats sing along with a tuneless croon,
We laugh as the dog joins in the song,
And bounces about like it's a cartoon.

The moon winks down with a silvery glow,
While shadows dance in the chilly air,
Counting our dreams as we giggle low,
By the old barn, down by the square.

Fireflies twinkle in winter's night,
Though they've packed up and gone somewhere,
Still we giggle, holding dreams so tight,
Wishing they'd come back, beyond compare!

The Warmth of Kindness by the Fire

Gather 'round, the fire's alive,
With marshmallows to toast, it's a sweet affair,
While grumpy Uncle Bob tries to thrive,
Telling tales that are quite beyond compare.

Cats on laps and noses aglow,
Grandma's stories of yesteryears,
She smiles as the tales start to flow,
And even the cat seems to catch our cheers.

The dog sneezes, and sparks take flight,
A race to hug before the warmth fades,
As holiday fun turns merry and bright,
Old socks as gifts?—Oh, what charades!

With every cheer, the night feels so right,
Jokes bounce like snowflakes through the gloom,
Together we laugh until we take flight,
In dreams of joy, love, and silly room!

Lanterns of Hope Along the Path

Beneath the twinkling stars so bright,
I tripped on my own scarf last night.
With lanterns glowing, the path was clear,
But my silly dance drew a forest deer.

I found a sock that just won't pair,
It waved at me as if to declare,
With every giggle from the shining lights,
I knew my hopes were taking flight.

The moon giggled as I misstepped,
While squirrels watched in bemused rep.
I tossed my hat into the air,
It landed on a snowman's stare!

So here's to laughter, mischief, and cheer,
And dreams that make our hearts sincere.
Every trip and fall, a tale to tell,
In the lantern glow, all is well.

Rainbow Lights in the Snow's Embrace

Over rooftops, lights are strung,
I tried to dance and fell, oh, sung!
The colors twinkled with such delight,
As I found myself in a snowball fight.

With every throw, my aim was weak,
A fluffy hit turns laughter peak.
While rainbows flashed in the frosty air,
My buddy's hat found a snowman's hair!

I wish for sweets, but lo, what's this?
A cookie monster's kiss? I'd not want to miss!
With giggles bouncing from tree to tree,
A powdered face with glee is me!

Funny moments fit the festive scene,
In snow's embrace, we share the sheen.
With each silly tale and joyful shout,
We find the magic swirling about.

The Harmony of Hearts Entwined

A jolly tune wafts through the air,
While I try to tango with my pet hare.
Missteps fly as we dance around,
Spinning with joy, both us and the ground.

With heart-shaped cookies, I made a mess,
In flour clouds, the critters confess.
They joined my party, furry and bright,
As laughter echoed through the night.

Each chirp and purr, a melody sweet,
Whiskers and tails in a festive beat.
We sang together, what a scene,
Caught up in mischief, such a dream!

In this jamboree, all's in sync,
Unexpected buddies made me think.
For in the laughter and mishaps found,
Harmony blooms where joy is unbound.

Silhouettes of Dreams in the Moonlight

Under moonlight's glow, a dance I share,
With shadows leaping without a care.
Every step echoes a silly waltz,
As I twirl and trip, oh, what a jolt!

The silhouettes sway like they're in tune,
With chipmunk cheers beneath the moon.
I lost my shoe—a comical plot,
While my cat grinned, claiming the spot.

Frisky figures in a frosty breeze,
Made laughable giggles and soft sneezes.
As I leap and laugh, the world spins wide,
Touching the light where warmth can hide.

With each twinkle from the night's embrace,
A whimsical smile found a place.
So here's to dreams that dance and glide,
In moonlit magic, joy our guide.

Tinsel Tangled in Laughter

Tinsel gleams on a tree, oh so bright,
Elves are giggling, what a sight!
Ornaments dance, hang by a thread,
One took a dive, now it's wed.

Gifts in a pile, looks like a mess,
Unwrapping magic in sheer excess.
Ribbons escape, twirling like sprites,
Who knew chaos could bring such delights?

Cookies are baking, a whimsical smell,
Santa's been sneaking, what a knell!
Milk's all gone, the reindeer squeal,
Wait till they see what's for their meal!

Snowflakes twirl in a frosty spree,
Chasing each other, just like me.
With laughter ringing, let's make a toast,
To a holiday we love the most!

Fireflies in the Frost

Fireflies flicker in the frosty air,
Dancing like dreams without a care.
Snowmen giggle, their noses askew,
They're planning a prank; who knew?

Snowballs fly with a wintery blast,
Footprints trace stories of the past.
Hot cocoa spills, marshmallows afloat,
Each sip brings giggles—oh what a joke!

Sledding down hills at a breakneck speed,
Who thought a twist would lead to a bead?
Laughter erupts, as we tumble and roll,
Winter is wild, it brightens the soul!

Fireflies buzzing, against the cold glow,
Whispers of magic in the fresh snow.
The night is a canvas, vibrant with cheer,
Here's to the laughter, let's all persevere!

Wishes Wrapped in a Bow

Wishes are nestled in boxes so neat,
Each one's a treasure, oh what a treat!
A cat in the corner thinks it's a game,
Threading through ribbons, oh such a claim!

Wrapping paper shreds dance on the floor,
As kids leap about, then giggle and roar.
"Whose gift is this?" they puzzledly shout,
Only to find it's a sock, no doubt!

Bows on the heads of the family dog,
He prances about, quite a festive hog.
With wagging tail and a jolly bark,
He's stealing the show, igniting a spark!

Unwrapping laughter is always the key,
For joy's in the mess, just wait and see.
As wishes unfold, and the smiles grow wide,
Joyful confusion, it cannot hide!

Frosted Memories of Yesteryear

Frosted windows dream of days gone by,
Chasing our shadows beneath the sky.
Each little flake holds a story or two,
Of giggles and snowball fights, who knew?

The old radio croons festive tunes,
As we dance in our socks, making merry goons.
A puppy spins wildly, chasing his tail,
Tangled in lights, oh what a tale!

Forgotten mittens are lost in the fray,
Yet every mishap brings joy come what may.
With each jolly tune and cheer all around,
Our hearts fill with laughter, love is profound.

So here's to the memories, fogged with delight,
Wrapped in the warmth of a cozy night.
We'll cherish these moments, both silly and dear,
For joy is the treasure we hold near!

An Ode to Hope in a Winter's Tale

Snowflakes dancing, oh so white,
Where's my cocoa? It feels just right.
The stockings hung, slightly askew,
Filled with goodies, and some old glue!

Reindeer giggles, they hit the roof,
I hope they left me some brand new proof.
A dance of jingle bells all around,
What's that sneaky elf making sound?

I chase the cat who's lost a toy,
Wrapped it up as a winter joy.
Laughter bubbles, socks on my head,
Is that my gift? Or catnip instead?

Oh, snowmen grinning, hats too big,
I'll sled down hills, come dance a jig.
In this tale with giggles galore,
Dreams are funny; who could ask for more?

The Call of the Hearth on a Chilly Night

The fire crackles, what a scene,
Pine cones pop, you know what I mean.
Grandma's cookies, still so warm,
Did I just eat that? Oh what charm!

The cat is prowling like a king,
Amidst the lights, he starts to cling.
A dance of shadows on the wall,
Who knew my aunt could trip and fall?

Hot chocolate flowing, whipped cream high,
I'll wear my marshmallow like a tie.
Kiddo's giggles, wrapping tight,
A funky beat beneath moonlight.

Tangled lights, oh what a sight,
Yet laughter makes the silly bright.
In cozy moments shared by all,
Such warmth within these winter's thrall.

Glowing Embers of Past and Future

A box of ornaments, neatly stacked,
Wait, is this one, or did I act?
Memories flicker like the flame,
Did Grandma really rhyme my name?

Tomorrow's plans, so bright and bold,
But first, some snacks wrapped tight in gold.
The cat's the star of every play,
Stealing treats in a sneaky way.

Old songs playing, off-key delight,
As silly dancing fills the night.
We giggle, trip, and jingle bells,
With stories shared that no one tells.

From silly wishes to future fun,
Let's hope there's laughter for everyone.
With twinkling leads, we dance and cheer,
In our hearts, this joy is clear.

A Soft Glow Amidst the Pines

In the forest where fur trees sigh,
Bubbles of laughter drift on by.
A squirrel stole my nutty snack,
Should I be angry, or just laugh back?

Spirits twinkle upon each limb,
While I start to lose my shiny whim.
Forgotten lights now tangled tight,
I'm a human puzzle, what a sight!

Snowflakes stumble as they land,
On my nose, quite unplanned.
Each glow around feels warm and bright,
Bringing giggles all through the night.

The whispers of the trees take flight,
Kisses from winter, oh what a sight!
Let's toast to moments, both silly and sweet,
With hopes and laughter, life is a treat.

A Night of Wonders Wrapped in Wonder

Jolly old elves dance with flair,
Socks on the ceiling, reindeer in air.
Gifts made of candy, toys made of cheese,
Laughter erupts, everyone's at ease.

Snowmen are sprightly, all dressed in style,
Doing the cha-cha, goofing a while.
With cookies for shimmying, milk for the team,
Who knew that the night could burst with such gleam?

Tinsel is tangled, a cat's new delight,
Rolling in ribbons, oh, what a sight!
In dreamland of giggles, we spin and twirl,
Each twinkling star beckons, let's dance and swirl!

Laughter wrapped up like a gift so bright,
Let's keep this magic, hold tight to the night.
With winks and with wiggles, we'll frolic till dawn,
In a night of true wonders, let's carry it on!

Chasing Starlight on Frosty Paths

Under the moonlight, we race in the chill,
Chasing our shadows up every hill.
Hot cocoa spills, what a spectacular mess,
Sleds zooming sideways, oh, what finesse!

Fuzzy mittens stuck unto snowballs,
Laughter erupts, OH the snowman falls!
Wishing for snowflakes to tickle our noses,
Maybe we'll see Santa—who knows where he dozes?

With marshmallows bouncing like sugary dreams,
The night gets a little more bursty, it seems.
We giggle and grapple, and slip, and we slide,
Winter's our playground, oh how we glide!

Counting the stars that tumble and twirl,
While we haphazardly give kindness a whirl.
Let's dance through the night with each frosty laugh,
On paths made of starlight, let's find our path!

Serenade of Snowflakes in the Night

Snowflakes are waltzing, they twirl and they dip,
Even the penguins are joining the trip.
Twirling in circles like frisky young pups,
Catching our breath in frosty hiccups.

Icicles shimmer like disco balls bright,
While snowmen debate if they'll dance through the night.

Elves gathering round for a wild, snowy treat,
With cocoa and giggles, oh how we repeat!

Whirling in wonder with hats that are silly,
Breath bubbles up, oh what a fun frilly!
Footprints in powder, our secrets to hide,
Creating a symphony, laughter as pride.

As stars wink above with an impish delight,
The serenade stretches, from dusk until bright.
Such joy in the air as we waltz with the cold,
This melody sparkles, never gets old!

Light the Way to Tomorrow's Wish

Candles are flickering, shadows take flight,
Whispering wishes that twinkle at night.
With each little glimmer, we giggle and cheer,
Maybe a dragon will swoop down from here!

Elf hats are floppy, and cookies abound,
We toss sprinkles everywhere round and round.
Making this magic a riotous fuse,
Shouting with glee as we choose and refuse!

With laughter that bubbles like soda pop spree,
Light spills from the tree as bright as can be.
Chasing our dreams on this whimsical ride,
With joy in our hearts and our friends by our side.

As clocks start to chime, we all raise a cheer,
To laughter and friendship, and a brand new year.
Light shapes the new wishes, fruitcake aside,
Let's dance through the night, and let joy be our guide!

Milton Keynes UK
Ingram Content Group UK Ltd.
UKHW021240191124
451300UK00007B/167

9 789916 940549